CHRISTMAS PRESENTS KIDS CAN MAKE

Kathy Ross

Illustrated by Sharon Lane Holm

The Millbroo   Connecticut

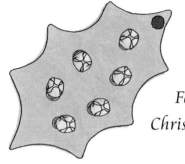

For my own little angel, Alli.—K.R.

For Joseph, Susan, and Brett—Thanks for all the
Christmas memories—S.L.H.

Library of Congress Cataloging-in-Publication Data
Ross, Kathy (Katharine Reynolds), 1948-
Christmas presents kids can make/ by Kathy Ross ; illustrated by Sharon Lane Holm.
p. cm.
ISBN 0-7613-1754-6 (lib. bdg.) –ISBN 0-7613-1482-2 (pbk.)
1. Christmas decorations—Juvenile literature. 2. Handicraft—Juvenile literature. 3. Gifts—
Juvenile literature. [1. Christmas decorations. 2. Handicraft. 3. Gifts.] I. Holm, Sharon Lane, ill.
II. Title.
TT900.C4 R674966 2001
745.5—dc21   00-046069

Published by The Millbrook Press, Inc.
2 Old New Milford Road
Brookfield, Connecticut 06804
www.millbrookpress.com

Contents

CHRISTMAS PRESENTS
KIDS CAN MAKE

Countdown to Christmas Tree

Make this Christmas tree to give as an early gift.

What you need:

lid from metal cookie tin

white glue

25 sequins of different shapes

green and red construction paper

hole punch

red ribbon or yarn

scissors

pretty trim about as wide as the rim of the lid

pen or pencil

red felt scrap

masking tape

strip of sticky-back magnet

6

What you do:

1 From the green construction paper, cut a Christmas-tree shape that will fit inside the lid of the metal cookie tin. Put a strip of masking tape down the center of the inside of the lid to create a better gluing surface. Glue the tree into the lid, attaching it to the masking-tape strip.

2 Cut a holder for the base of the tree from the red felt. Glue the holder to the base of the tree. Decorate the holder with trim.

3 Tear a long strip of masking tape in half lengthwise. Cover the inside rim of the lid with the strips. They will help the glue hold.

4 Cut a 12-inch (30-cm) length of red construction paper, making it narrow enough to fit inside the rim of the metal lid. Write the numbers from 1 to 25 across the strip. Glue the strip to the rim below the tree. Glue trim around the rest of the inner rim.

5 Cut a 10-inch (25-cm) length of thin red ribbon or yarn. Put a piece of masking tape on the back of the lid behind the top of the tree. Glue the two ends of the red ribbon or yarn to the masking-tape strip and cover it with more masking-tape strips to secure it.

6 Use the hole punch to punch twenty-five holes from the magnet strip. Peel the paper off each dot and stick it to a sequin. The magnet dot will allow each sequin to stick to the tin lid. Place a sequin over each number on the paper strip.

To use the countdown tree, hang it up, and, starting on December 1, trim the tree with one sequin ornament each day. When all the ornaments are on the tree it will be December 25. Merry Christmas!

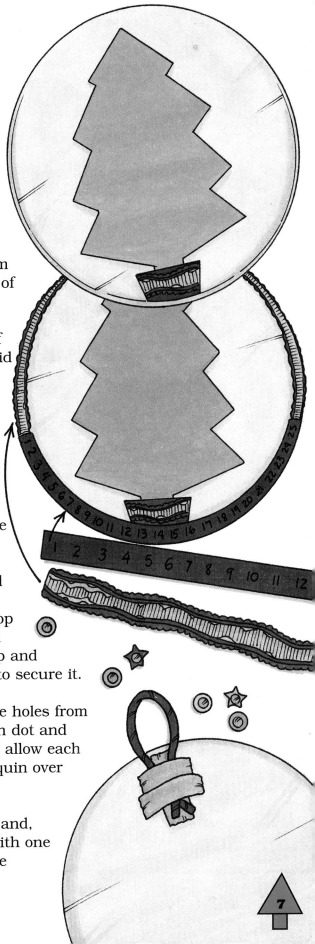

7

Christmas Wreath Hanger

Here is a gift to make that is both useful and pretty.

What you need:

thin wire hanger

six or more 12-inch (30-cm) red pipe cleaners

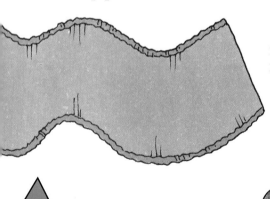

fat green ribbon or fabric strip for bow

scissors

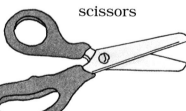

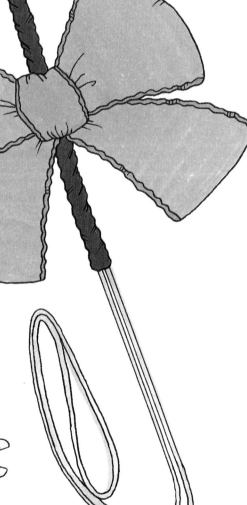

What you do:

1 Pull the center bottom wire of the coat hanger down to pull the sides together. Fold the bottom of the hanger up about 4 inches (10 cm), then fold it up again, about in half, to make a hook to hang a wreath on.

2 Bend the hook at the top of the hanger to face the opposite direction of the hook at the bottom.

3 Using the red pipe cleaners, wrap from the top hook to just above the tip of the wreath hook.

4 Tie a pretty bow from the ribbon or fabric strip. Use a piece of pipe cleaner to attach the bow to the pipe-cleaner-wrapped portion of the hanger.

The lucky person who receives this hanger can hook this over a door and be all ready to hang a holiday wreath.

Jingle Bell Bracelet

Put someone special you know in the Christmas spirit with this holiday bracelet.

What you need:

bright color sock with a stretchy cuff

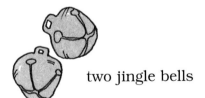

green sparkle stem

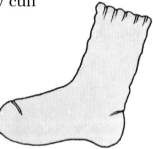

two jingle bells

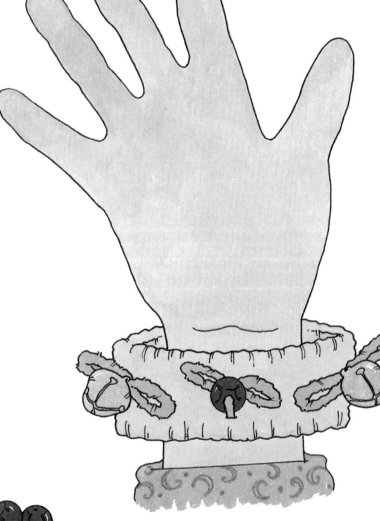

two red beads

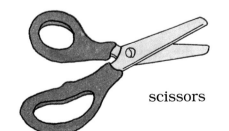

scissors

What you do:

1 To make the bracelet, cut a 1-inch (2.5-cm)-wide band from the top of the cuff of the sock.

2 Cut four 2-inch (5-cm) pieces of green sparkle stem.

3 Thread one end of a sparkle stem piece down through the weave of the sock and up again to fasten it to the sock. Thread a jingle bell onto the sparkle stem, then twist the two ends together to secure the bell to the sock bracelet. Do the same thing on the other side of the bracelet.

4 Between the bells on each side of the bracelet thread another piece of sparkle stem. Slide a red bead on each of these and twist the ends together to hold each bead in place.

5 You might want to trim the ends of the sparkle stems so that they are all about the same length.

Try making more than one of these bracelets in different colors. You might also have other ideas for what decorations you attach. These bracelets can be worn on ankles as well as wrists. Whoever you give them to will look and sound very Christmasy!

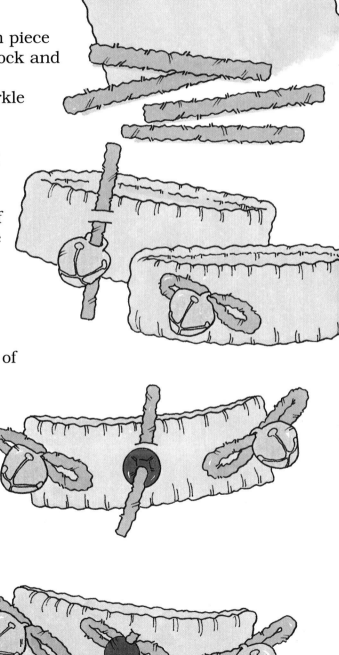

Marker Cap Lapel Pin

Here is just the gift to make for your favorite aunt!

What you need:

colorful cap from discarded fat marker

small artificial flowers

jingle bell

masking tape

white glue

safety pin

thin wire

narrow ribbon

scissors

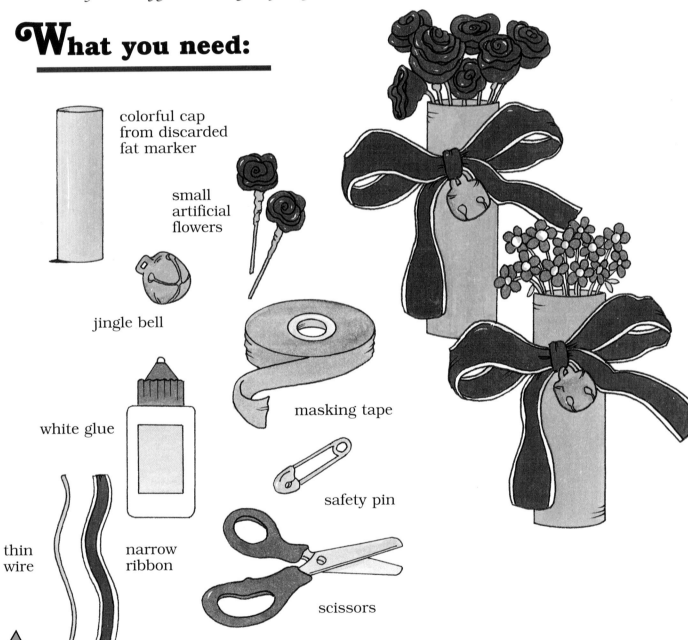

What you do:

1 Turn the marker cap so that the opening is on the top to form a little container for the flowers. Put a small piece of masking tape just above the middle of one side of the marker cap.

2 Glue the back of the closed safety pin to the tape and secure it over the glue with another piece of masking tape. This will be the back of the lapel pin.

3 Cut an 8-inch (20-cm) length of ribbon. Thread one end of the ribbon through the closed safety pin on the back of the marker cap. Tie the ribbon in a pretty bow. Trim the ends as needed.

4 To attach the jingle bell to the bow, thread a piece of wire through the top of the jingle bell and under the bow. Tie the two ends of the wire together to secure the bell. Trim off the ends of the wire.

5 If necessary, trim the stems of the flowers to make them fit nicely in the marker cap container. Squeeze some glue into the container. Arrange the flowers in the container by adjusting the ends in the glue.

When the glue has dried you will have a lovely lapel pin. You might want to make more than one of this simple but attractive holiday gift.

Snowman Antenna Ball

*This is the perfect gift for anyone who has trouble
finding his or her car in a crowded mall parking lot.*

What you need:

2-inch (5-cm)
Styrofoam ball

child's sock

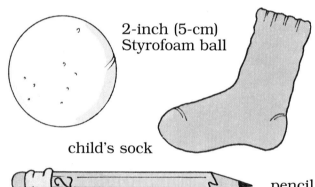

pencil

colored
map pins

big sequin or
button

straight pins

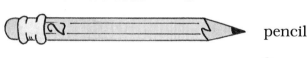

scissors

tiny red
pom-pom

white glue

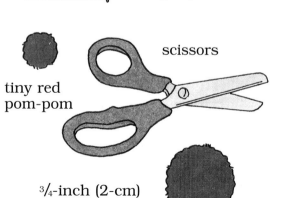

³/₄-inch (2-cm)
red pom-pom

What you do:

1 Cut the foot off the sock, leaving the heel end with the cuff. This will be a hat for the Styrofoam ball head.

2 Roll the cut end of the foot up at least twice to make a band on the hat. Roll the end until the hat is about 2½ inches (6 cm) long.

3 Put the hat on the Styrofoam ball and secure it with straight pins. Because the car antenna will need to go through the center of the ball to attach it, put all the pins in at an angle so they do not cross the center of the ball and block the way of the antenna.

4 Glue the larger red pom-pom to the end of the hat. Use a map pin to attach a pretty sequin or button to the band of the hat to decorate it.

5 Stick two map pins in the Styrofoam ball below the brim of the hat for eyes. Attach the tiny red pom-pom with a straight pin for the nose.

6 Use the point of the pencil to poke a small hole through the bottom of the head to show where the antenna should go.

A snowman antenna ball is not only a practical gift but a fun one as well.

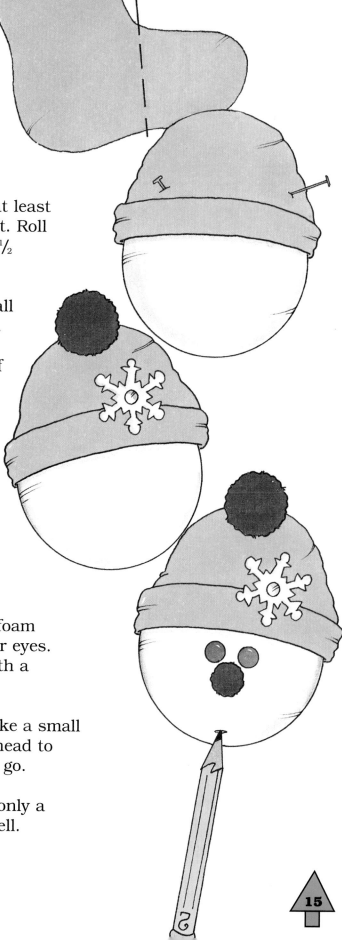

Decorated Hair Clip

Wow! What a gift! Designer hair clips by you!

What you need:

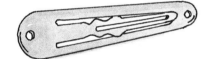

bend-to-close hair clip

fine jewelry craft wire

three pretty buttons

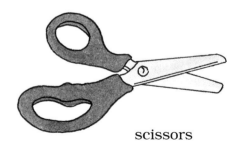

 seed beads

scissors

What you do:

1 Choose three pretty buttons that look well together. They can all be the same or all different. You are the designer.

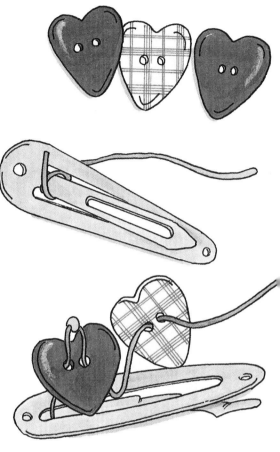

2 Cut a 6-inch (15-cm) piece of fine wire. Tie one end of the wire to the closed end of the hair clip.

3 Pop the clip open. Thread the first button onto the wire by threading the end of the wire through the back of the button. If you want, you can add a seed bead on top of the button before threading the wire down through the second hole in the button. If your button is a shank button (one with a loop on the back), you will not be able to add a bead to that button.

4 Add another button following the same procedure. Do not make the wire so tight that the clip is unable to open and close. Check to make sure it will still work after adding each button. Continue until all buttons are used.

5 When you have secured all three buttons to the top of the clip, tie off the end of the wire and trim it.

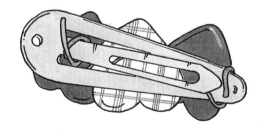

Ta Da! Your very own designer hair clip to give to someone special in your life.

Padded Envelope Trivet

A festive trivet would be a welcome gift for anyone's holiday table.

What you need:

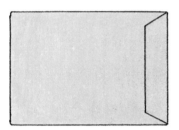

8½ - by 11-inch
(22- by 28-cm)
padded envelope

two 9- by 12-inch
(23- by 30-cm) felt pieces
of the same color

blue glue
gel

rickrack trim

scissors

stapler

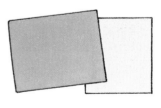

felt scraps in
other colors

What you do:

1 If the envelope has been used, pull out any staples and trim the open end so that it is straight across if necessary.

2 Set the padded envelope in the center of one of the felt pieces so that the edge of the felt shows all around the outside of the envelope. Set the second felt piece over the envelope and exactly matching the edges of the bottom felt piece. Staple the two felt pieces together all around the edges with the envelope in between them. The best way to do this is to put one staple in the center of each end, then one in the center of each side to hold the envelope in place between the felt pieces. Then go back and staple the open areas around the trivet.

3 Decorate the trivet by gluing rickrack all around the edges over the staples.

4 Cut one or more pretty holiday shapes from the felt scraps to glue in one corner of the trivet.

You can make a whole set of trivets using a different-size padded envelope for each one.

Priority Mail Box Video Holder

A small priority mail carton is just the right size for storing a special Christmas video.

What you need:

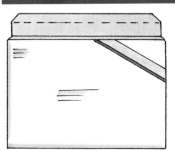

6- by 9- by 2-inch
(15- by 23- by 5-cm)-
size priority mail box

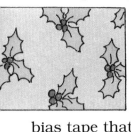

fabric

white
glue

bias tape that goes
with the fabric

two paper
fasteners

thin ribbon

scissors

paintbrush

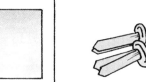

Styrofoam tray or egg
carton for drying

masking
tape

newspaper
to work on

What you do:

1 You will need an unused priority mail box. These boxes are free at the post office and come flat. Leave the box flat until after you have covered it with fabric. Do not remove the white strip on the flap of the box. Cut a piece of fabric big enough to cover the outside of the box. It does not have to fit exactly. You can trim the edges after the glue dries. Cut a slit in the fabric on each side where there is a slit in the box to slip the tabs in to assemble.

2 Cover the outer surface of the box with strips of masking tape to create a better gluing surface. You do not have to cover the entire surface. A few crisscrossed pieces of tape over each section of the box will be fine.

3 Cover the entire outside of the box with glue, using the paintbrush to spread it evenly. Carefully set the fabric on the box over the glue, making sure it is as smooth as possible and the slits in the fabric are lined up with the slits in the box. Put the box on the Styrofoam tray or egg carton to dry. This will keep it from sticking to the newspaper.

4 When the project is dry, trim off the extra fabric.

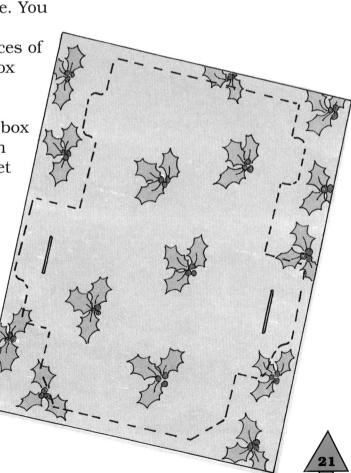

Assemble the box and secure the sides and tabs with glue.

Finish the edges of the box by gluing on bias tape.

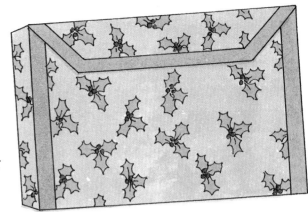

Poke a hole in the center of the flap. Hold the flap closed and poke another hole about 1 inch (2.5 cm) below the center of the closed flap. Put a paper fastener in each hole and secure it by bending the two arms in opposite directions.

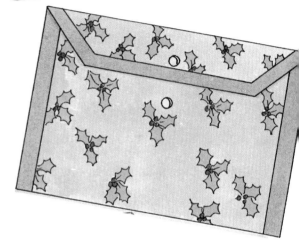

Cut a 10-inch (25-cm) length of ribbon. Tie the ribbon around the paper fastener on the flap of the box. Close the flap and tie the ribbon in a knot, then a bow, around the second paper fastener. The ribbon should be able to slip on and off the second fastener to open and close the box.

This is a great gift for the video taker in your family. This year's Christmas video can be stored in the video holder, ready to be enjoyed next Christmas.

Decorated Tape Dispenser

*Just about anyone would find this
decorated tape dispenser an attractive
and useful holiday gift.*

What you need:

new roll of cellophane tape
in a clear plastic dispenser

white
glue

Styrofoam tray
to work on

small mixed
sequins

What you do:

1 Remove the roll of tape from
the dispenser and set aside.
Take out the paper insert and
discard.

2 Cover the back inside of the
plastic tape dispenser with
white glue. Cover the glue with
assorted sequins.

3 Leave the dispenser laying flat on
the Styrofoam tray until the glue
dries completely. This could take
as long as a week.

4 When the glue is dry, put the tape
back in the dispenser.

Can you think of other ways to decorate the inside of the tape
dispenser? Maybe some holiday wrapping paper or colored glue?

23

Stuffed Snowman Friend

Here is a project sure to delight your younger brother or sister.

What you need:

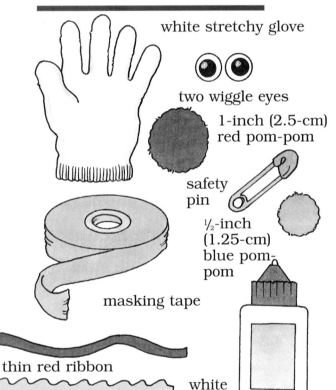

white stretchy glove

two wiggle eyes

1-inch (2.5-cm) red pom-pom

safety pin

½-inch (1.25-cm) blue pom-pom

masking tape

thin red ribbon

thin trim or rickrack

white glue

scissors

fiberfill

thin string or yarn

two candy canes

What you do:

1 Turn the middle finger of the glove inside out up inside the glove. The two fingers on each side of the missing finger will become legs of the snowman, the thumb and little finger will become arms, and the hand portion will form the body and head. Stuff the entire snowman with fiberfill.

2 Cut a 10-inch (25-cm) length of ribbon. Tie it around the hand portion of the glove just above the thumb to form the neck of the snowman. Tie the ribbon in a pretty bow and trim the ends.

3 Cut a 6-inch (15-cm) piece of thin string or yarn. Tie the top of the glove closed about 1 inch (2.5 cm) below the cuff. Trim off the ends of the yarn. Fold the cuff down to form a hat for the snowman.

4 Glue trim around the brim of the hat. Glue the red pom-pom to the top of the hat. Put small squares of masking tape on the head of the snowman where you want to glue the eyes and the nose. Put a square of masking tape on the back of each wiggle eye and glue them in place. Put a piece of masking tape on one side of the blue pom-pom and glue the tape side to the snowman to make the nose.

5 Tie two candy canes together with a piece of the thin red ribbon. Use the safety pin to pin the snowman's hands together. Slip the candy canes behind the pinned hands to look like the snowman is holding them.

Slip a piece of yarn through the ribbon at the back of the snowman and tie the two ends together to make a hanger if you would like this snowman to hang on the tree.

Decorated Wrapped Coins

Here is a fun way to give the gift of money.

What you need:

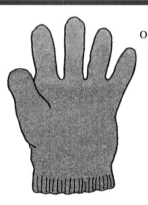

old knit stretchy glove

full package of wrapped
pennies (or other coins)

white glue

felt scrap

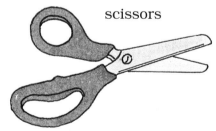

scissors   two tiny wiggle eyes

two tiny pom-poms

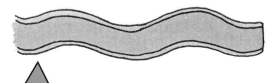

¹/₂-inch (1.25-cm) wide ribbon

What you do:

1 Cut a piece a little more than 1 inch (2.5 cm) long off the tip of the thumb of the glove. Roll the cut end of the tip up to form the brim of a little hat. Glue the hat to one end of the wrapped coins. Glue one of the tiny pom-poms to the top of the hat.

2 Glue the two wiggle eyes on the side of the wrapper just below the hat brim. Glue the second pom-pom on below the eyes for a nose.

3 Cut the longest finger off the glove. Cut the tip off the finger so you have a knit tube. Slip the tube over the wrapped coins to make clothes.

4 Fold the felt scrap in half and cut an oval shape at an angle 1½ inches (4 cm) long with one end on the fold. Open the oval up and glue it to the bottom of the wrapper with the two oval halves sticking out from the front to look like feet.

5 Cut a 6-inch (15-cm) length of ribbon. Tie the ribbon around the wrapper just below the nose to look like a scarf.

If you have any siblings or baby-sitters in college, a roll of quarters for the washing machines makes a great gift.

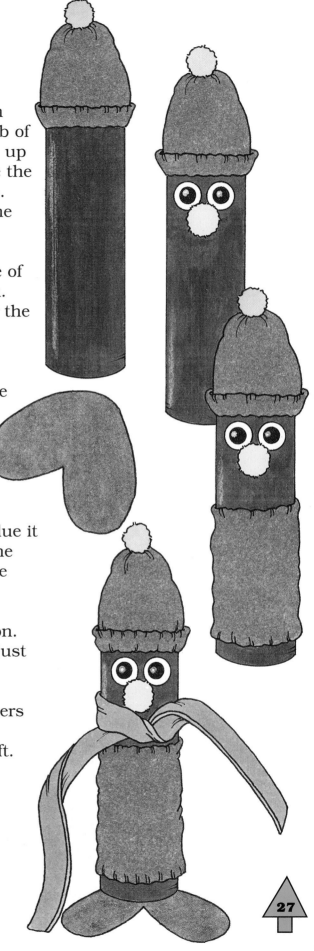

Holiday Stamp Holder

This idea for a holiday stamp holder can be used
to make stamp dispensers for any time of the year.

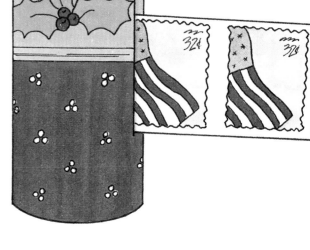

What you need:

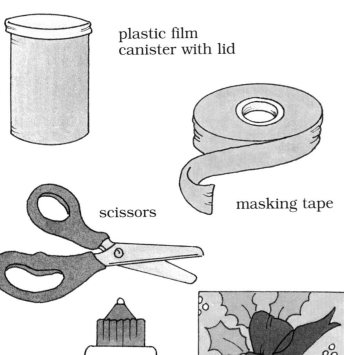

plastic film
canister with lid

scissors

masking tape

tiny sequins
and glitter

white
glue

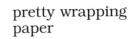

pretty wrapping
paper

What you do:

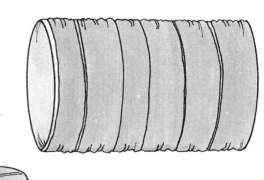

1 Cover the outer surface of the film canister with masking tape to create a better gluing surface. Cover the top of the lid with tape also.

2 Cut a slit about three quarters of the way down the side of the canister.

3 Cut a piece of wrapping paper to fit around the canister to cover it. Glue the paper over the canister with the two ends meeting at the slit so that the slit is left open.

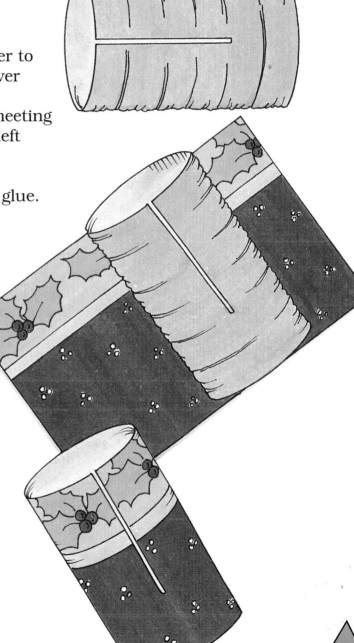

4 Cover the top of the lid with glue. Sprinkle the glue with the sequins. Dust with glitter to help fill in any gaps.

To use the dispenser, just slip a roll of stamps in the canister with the end of the roll sticking out of the slit in the side. Snap the top on the canister. As stamps are needed, the roll can be pulled out from the side of the canister.

Milkweed Pod Ornament

If you collect some dry milkweed pods in the late fall you can make very pretty ornaments to give as gifts.

What you need:

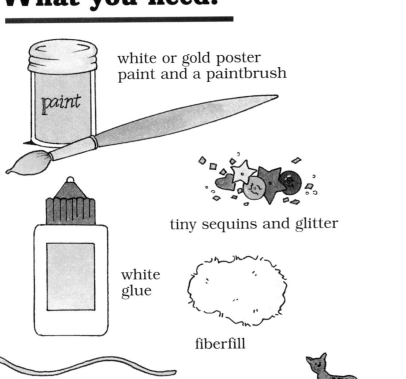

white or gold poster paint and a paintbrush

tiny sequins and glitter

white glue

fiberfill

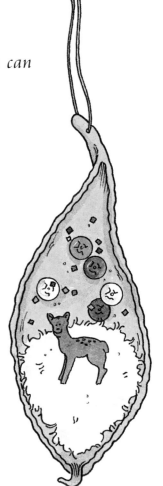

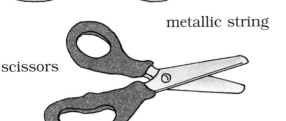

metallic string

scissors

tiny plastic figure

milkweed pod

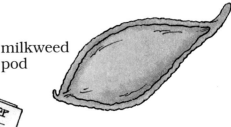

newspaper to work on

What you do:

1 Paint the entire pod and let it dry.

2 Poke a tiny hole in the narrow end of the pod. Cut a 6-inch (15-cm) piece of metallic thread. String one end of the thread through the hole and tie the two ends together for a hanger.

3 Cover the inside of the pod with glue. Glue a little fiberfill in the bottom for snow. Glue a tiny plastic or paper figure standing in the snow. Sprinkle sequins and glitter in the glue above the scene.

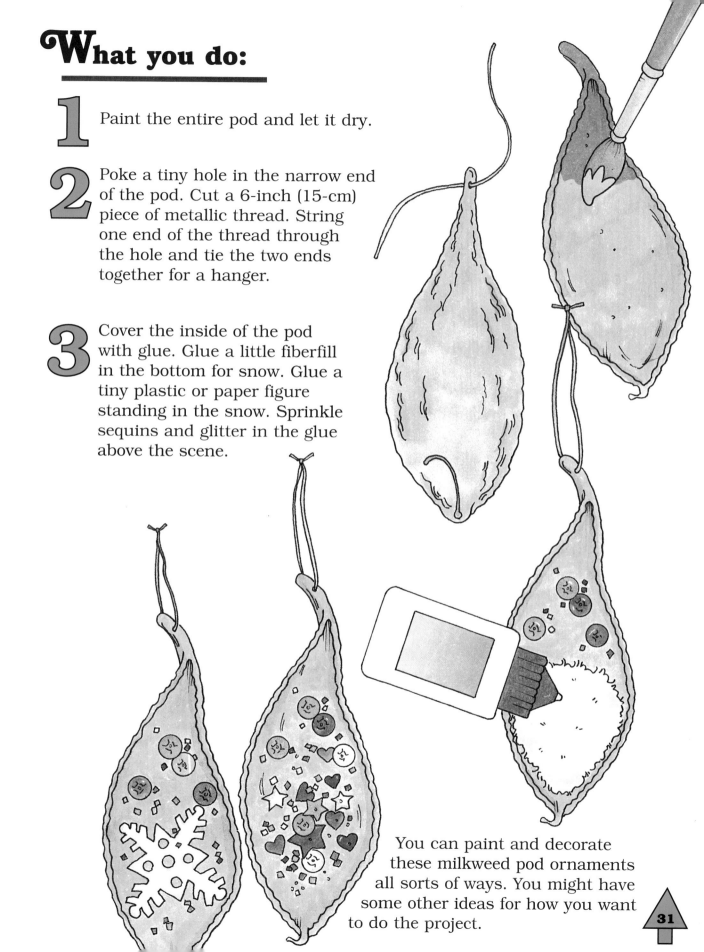

You can paint and decorate these milkweed pod ornaments all sorts of ways. You might have some other ideas for how you want to do the project.

Sticker Star Tree Pin

This tiny tree looks great worn on a coat.

What you need:

gold sticker stars

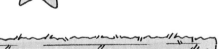

piece of gold sparkle stem

pin back or safety pin

white glue

plastic wrap

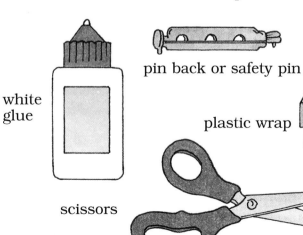

scissors

masking tape

What you do:

1 Use a squeeze bottle of glue to draw a small triangle shape in the plastic wrap. Make it a little over 1 inch (2.5 cm) wide at the base and 2 inches (5 cm) tall. Fill in the triangle shape with glue.

2 Use the gold sticker stars to make a tree, starting at the bottom and working up to the point.

3 Cut a ½-inch (1.25-cm) piece of the sparkle stem. Stick one end of the piece in the glue at the center of the bottom of the tree to form the base. Let the glue dry completely on a flat surface, undisturbed.

4 When the glue has dried, peel the tree off the plastic wrap. Use the scissors to trim off any excess glue that has run off the sides around the stars.

5 Put a small piece of masking tape on the back of the tree to create a better gluing surface. Glue on a safety pin or pin back. Put another piece of masking tape over the back of the safety pin or pin back to hold it in place while the glue dries.

You might want to make your tree with green stars or all different colors. How pretty!

33

Jingle Bell Hair Snaps

These hair snaps look and sound like Christmas!

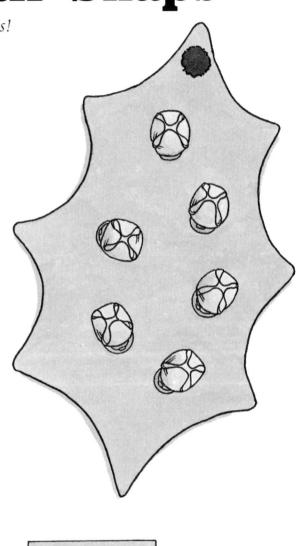

What you need:

6 snaps
(size no. 1/0
work well)

spool
of fine
wire

six jingle bells

white glue

scissors

small red
pom-pom

tiny hole punch

green construction paper

What you do:

1 Cut a 6-inch (15-cm) piece of wire. Unsnap a snap. Tie one end of the wire through the top part of the snap.

2 Thread a jingle bell onto the wire. Thread the wire down through another hole in the snap. Weave the wire in and out of the holes in the snap a few times to secure the bell. Tie off the end of the wire and trim off any extra. Use the top half of six snaps to make six jingle bell snaps.

3 For gift giving, make something pretty to attach the bells to. One idea is to cut a 4-inch (10-cm) holly leaf from the green construction paper.

4 Glue the red pom-pom to one point to look like a holly berry.

5 Punch a hole in the leaf for each hair snap you made. Attach the hair snaps to the holly by joining the top and bottom of each snap together through a hole in the leaf.

Each jingle bell hair snap can easily be snapped onto a lock of hair for a charming and musical holiday hair decoration.

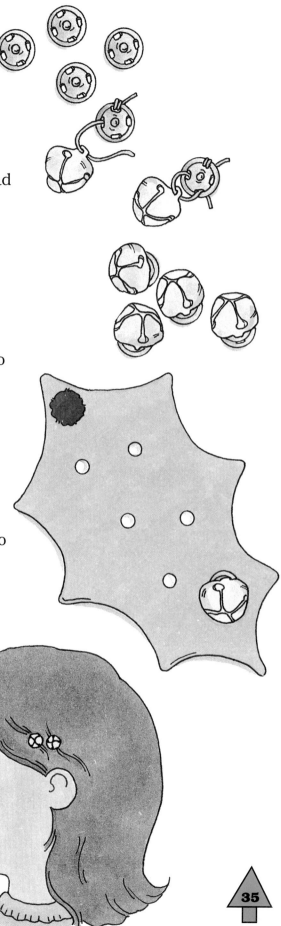

35

Beaded Spoon

Brighten up someone's holiday table with this attractive project.

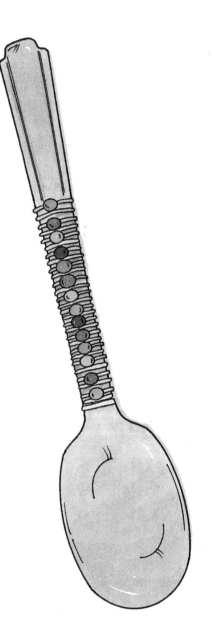

What you need:

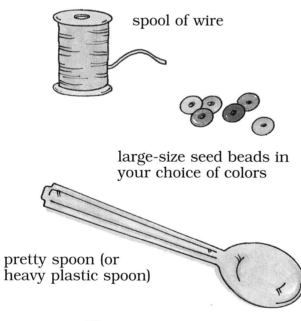

spool of wire

large-size seed beads in your choice of colors

pretty spoon (or heavy plastic spoon)

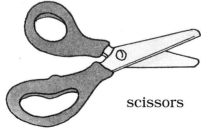

scissors

What you do:

1 Cut off a 16-inch (41-cm) piece of wire. How much you actually need will depend on the size of your spoon and how much of the handle you decide to decorate.

2 Wrap one end of the wire around the top of the spoon handle, just below the bowl, to secure the wire to the top of the spoon.

3 Thread a bead onto the wire so that it rests on the front of the handle. Wrap the wire snugly around the handle a couple of times, then add another bead. Continue to do this until about half the handle is decorated. If you go further, the decoration will interfere with the use of the spoon.

4 Trim off any extra wire and tuck the end under the wrapped wire to secure.

The colorful seed beads turn an ordinary spoon into a beautiful gift.

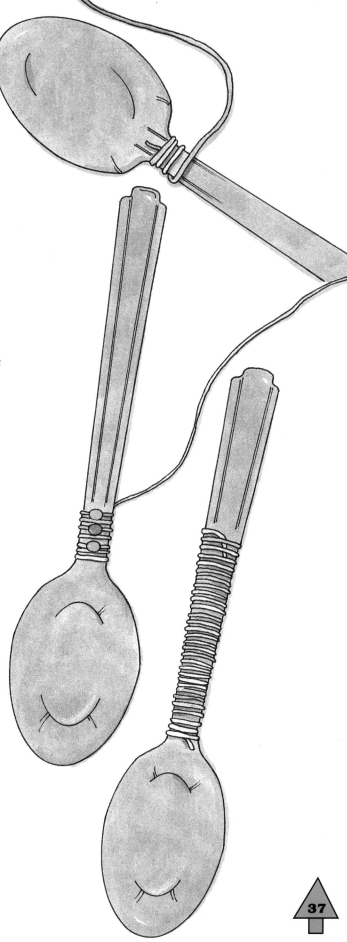

Envelope Coupon Keeper

For an extra surprise, collect some coupons to put into the coupon keeper before you give it as a gift.

What you need:

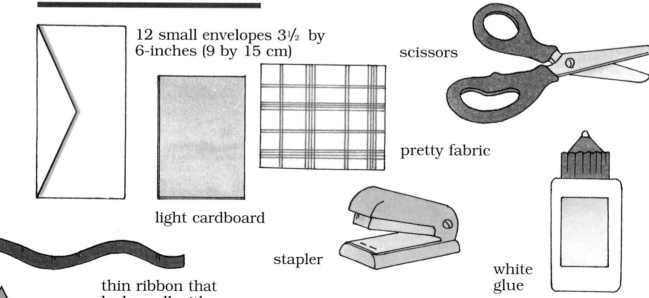

12 small envelopes 3½ by 6-inches (9 by 15 cm)

light cardboard

pretty fabric

scissors

stapler

white glue

thin ribbon that looks well with the fabric

What you do:

1 Cut the flaps off the twelve envelopes and stack them all facing in the same direction. Glue the envelopes together by covering the bottom two-thirds of the surface between each envelope with a thin coating of glue. Let the glue dry.

2 Cut an 8-inch (20-cm)-square piece of the light cardboard. Cut a 10-inch (25-cm) square of fabric. Place the cardboard in the fabric square. Fold the sides in and secure them using the stapler.

3 Fold the fabric-covered cardboard in half with the fabric on the outside. If you wish, you can glue a strip of ribbon across the long end on each side of the cardboard.

4 Cut a 2-foot (61-cm) length of ribbon. Center the ribbon in the folded cardboard so the two ends stick out of the front and the back of the folder.

5 Cover the outside of the front and back stack of envelopes with glue. Slide it into the fabric-covered cardboard with the open ends up to hold coupons. Push the envelopes to the bottom fold of the cardboard and over the fold in the ribbon. Make sure the ribbon is straight on both sides of the holder and coming out at the center on each side.

6 Tie the coupon keeper shut and let the glue dry.

The envelopes the bank uses to put money in will also work well for making this coupon file.

Tissue Box Angel

Turn an ordinary tissue box into a pretty Christmas angel for an extra-special gift.

What you need:

new square box of tissues

white coffee filter

aluminum foil

metallic trim

golf tee

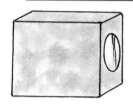

big red sequin

white glue

yarn bits for hair

markers

scissors

12-inch (30-cm) pipe cleaner in same shade as construction paper

masking tape

two holly leaf sequins

construction paper in skin tone of your choice

What you do:

1 Tear off a square of aluminum foil. Fold it in half and cut out a wing shape on the fold about 7 inches (18 cm) tall and 5 inches (13 cm) wide. Open the foil so you have two wings attached at the center. Put a piece of masking tape across the back center of the wings. This helps make a better gluing surface.

2 Turn the tissue box on its side so that the tissue hangs down one side. Put a strip of masking tape above the opening. Glue the wings on the box above the opening.

3 Cut the coffee filter in half. Fold each piece into thirds for the sleeves of the angel. Slide a sleeve on each end of the pipe cleaner, pointed end first, until they meet at the center. Glue the bottom of each sleeve together. Glue the sleeves over the center of the wings.

4 Cut a 2-inch (5-cm) circle from the construction paper. Use the markers to draw on a face. Glue on yarn bits for hair. Glue the holly leaves and red sequin berry in the angel hair. You can also cut the holly decoration from paper. Glue the head in the center of the wings and sleeves.

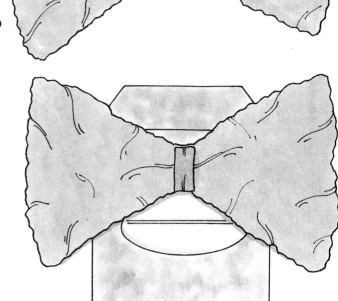

Fold the two sleeves toward the center of the angel. Wrap the two ends of the pipe cleaner around the golf tee to look like the angel has a trumpet.

 Glue metallic trim on each sleeve to decorate them.

This angel tissue box sits on the edge of a shelf with the tissue dress hanging down. When one tissue is removed, another will appear until the box is empty. What a lovely way to decorate a tissue box for the Christmas season!

Zipper Pull

Whoever gets this little treasure will jingle through the rest of the winter.

What you need:

jingle bell

¼-inch (0.6-cm) beads

sparkle stem

paper clip

What you do:

1 Pull the outer end of the paper clip away from the side slightly. String a jingle bell onto the paper clip so that it hangs from the bottom.

2 Wrap the paper clip with a piece of sparkle stem, stringing on one or two beads as you go. Do not wrap the outer end of the paper clip. This will be used to attach the pull to a zipper.

To attach the zipper pull, slip the outer end of the paper clip through the hole in the zipper and bend the clip slightly to keep it from slipping off.

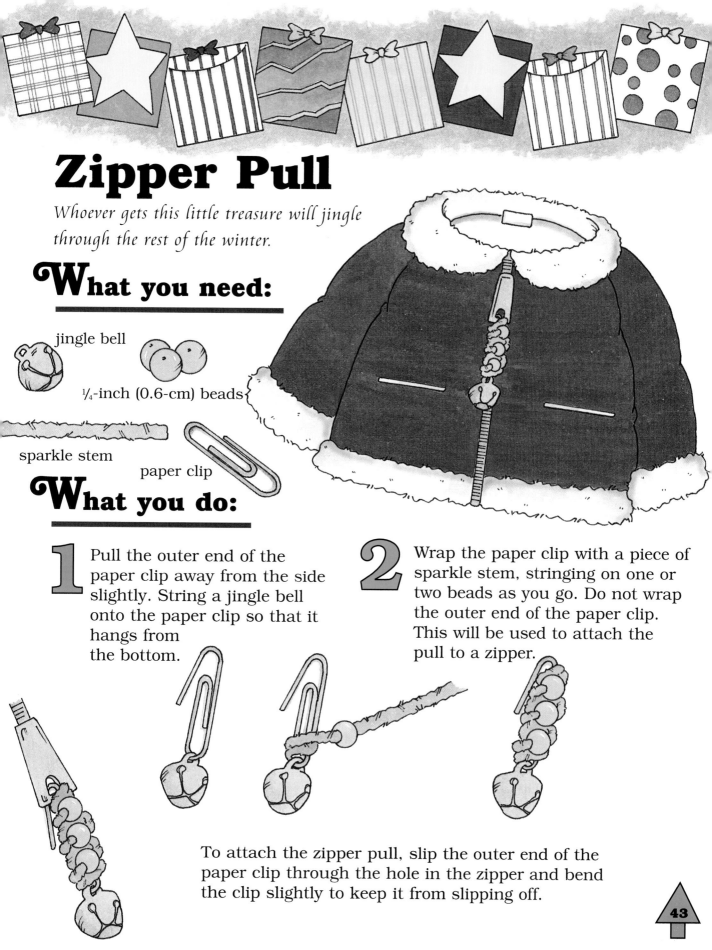

Paw Pads

Have you made a Christmas present for your favorite dog friend yet?

What you need:

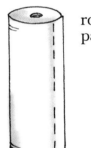 roll of white paper towels

 jingle bell

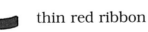 thin red ribbon

scissors

 stapler

 black marker

What you do:

1 Tear off ten strips of three attached paper towels. Stack the ten strips, making sure the edges are even with one another.

2 Cut a 3-foot (91-cm) length of red ribbon. Put the ribbon across the center of the middle paper towel stack and fold the towels in half over the ribbon. Tie the two ends of the ribbon together to make a hanger for the towels. Thread a jingle bell onto one end of the ribbon and then tie it in a bow.

3 Staple the front and back paper towels together on each side just below the ribbon hanger.

4 Use the black marker to decorate the top half paper towel on one side of the stack. Write "Paw Pads" and draw some muddy footprints.

Hang this pet gift by the door. It can come in very handy when a favorite pooch comes in muddy.

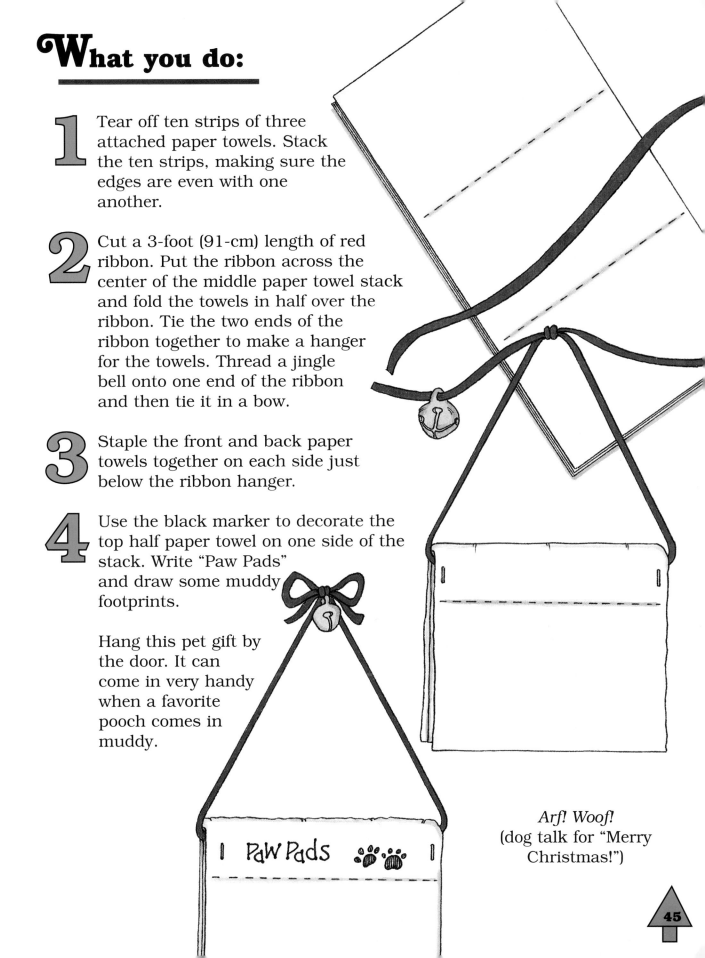

Paw Pads

Arf! Woof!
(dog talk for "Merry Christmas!")

Christmas Cat Collar

Kitty cat wants a Christmas present, too!

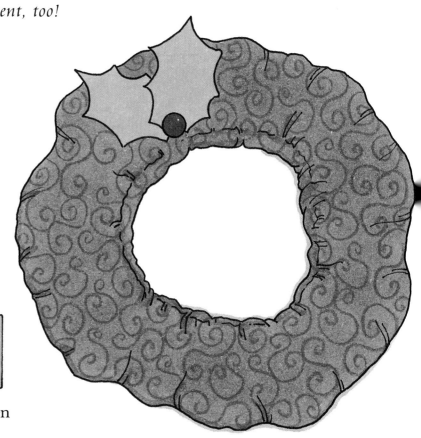

What you need:

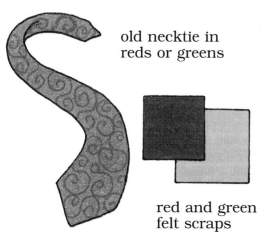

old necktie in reds or greens

red and green felt scraps

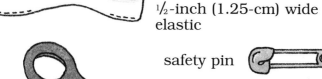

½-inch (1.25-cm) wide elastic

safety pin

scissors

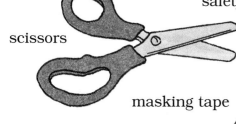

masking tape

blue glue gel

What you do:

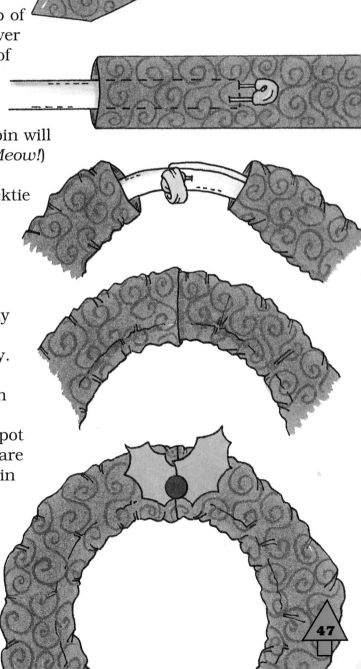

1 Cut a piece of elastic long enough to fit loosely around the cat's neck and overlap 1 inch (2.5 cm). Do not stretch the elastic at all.

2 Cut the narrow half of the necktie off. Cut off the point at the end.

3 Put a safety pin on one end of the elastic. Use the pin as a holder to thread the elastic through the strip of necktie. Gather the necktie strip over the elastic, then pin the two ends of the elastic together, overlapping the ends about 1 inch (2.5 cm). Wrap the safety-pinned ends with masking tape to be sure the pin will not open and poke the kitty cat. (*Meow!*)

4 Fold one of the cut ends of the necktie strip inside itself to create a clean edge. If the seam is coming unraveled secure it with a small amount of glue. Slip the folded end of the strip over the other end and glue it in place. Do not use any more glue then you need to because necktie fabric stains easily.

5 Cut two holly leaves from the green felt. Cut a holly berry from the red felt. Glue the two leaves over the spot where the two ends of the necktie are glued together. Glue the red berry in the center top of the two leaves.

This little gift will have kitty looking her Christmas best! *Meow! Purr!* (You guessed it! Kitty talk for "Merry Christmas!")

47

Catalog Christmas Tree

Here is a great way to use some of those
Christmas catalogs that come in the mail.

What you need:

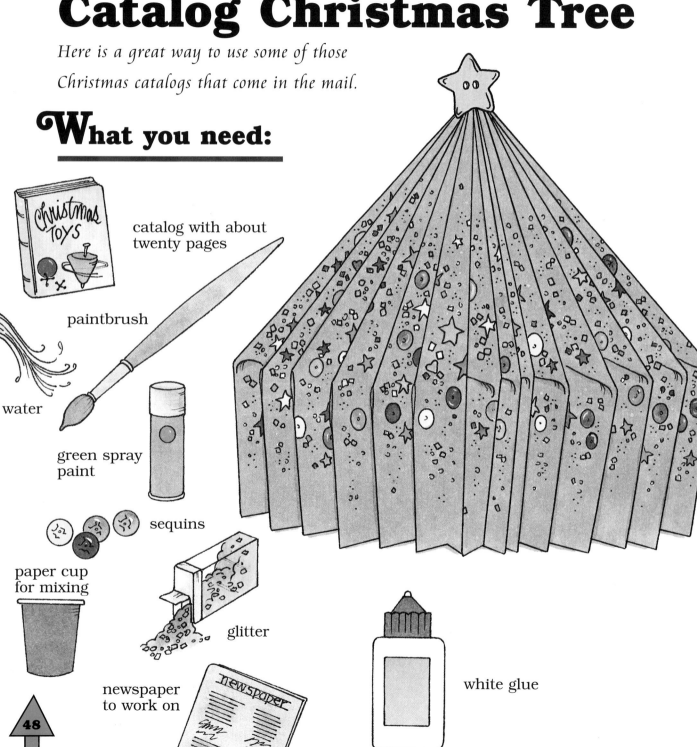

catalog with about
twenty pages

paintbrush

water

green spray
paint

sequins

paper cup
for mixing

glitter

newspaper
to work on

white glue

What you do:

1 Fold the top corner of the inside cover of the catalog down in a triangle to the inside center of the catalog. Fold the top corner of the back cover in to the center of the catalog.

2 Fold the top corner of each page of the catalog down to the center of the catalog, making sure you fold each page on the same side. When you are done folding, you will have a nice triangle-shaped tree that will stand by itself.

3 Because so many catalogs have shiny pages, poster paint is not a good choice for this project. It will peel off most catalogs, making quite a mess. It is best to ask an adult to help you spray-paint the tree green. Spray paint must be either done by an adult or with adult supervision.

4 When the paint has dried, you can decorate the tree. Mix two parts glue with one part water in the paper cup. Paint the front of the tree with the watery glue, then sprinkle it with sequins and glitter. If you do not have a large star-shaped sequin for the top, make a star from cut paper. Cover it with glitter to make it shiny, then glue it to the top of your tree.

The size of your tree will depend on the size of the catalog it is made from. One or more of these sturdy trees will make a lovely table display that will be enjoyed for many Christmas holidays to come.

Baby's First Christmas Ornament

This ornament makes a sweet memento for a new baby.

What you need:

white paper napkin

green paper scrap

red sequin

thin red ribbon

jingle bell

stapler

marker

white glue

hole punch

scissors

What you do:

1 Fold a paper napkin square into a triangle. Pull the two ends off the long side of the triangle together, then fold the last corner up over it, just like a folded diaper. Hold the three corners together with a staple.

2 Cut two holly leaves from the green paper. Glue them over the staple at the front of the diaper. Glue a red sequin over the center of the two leaves for a holly berry.

3 Cut a 2-inch (5-cm)-square piece of green paper. Use the marker to write "Baby's First Christmas" and the year on the paper. Punch a hole in the corner of the paper. Also punch a hole on one side of the diaper.

4 Cut a 6-inch (15-cm) length of ribbon. Thread one end through the hole in the diaper, then tie the two ends together to form a hanger. Thread a jingle bell and the paper onto one of the tied ribbon ends, then tie the ends in a knot around the bell and the paper to hold them in place.

You can use a colored or printed napkin for this project, too.

Rag Christmas Tree

I bet your teacher would love this little tree ornament.

What you need:

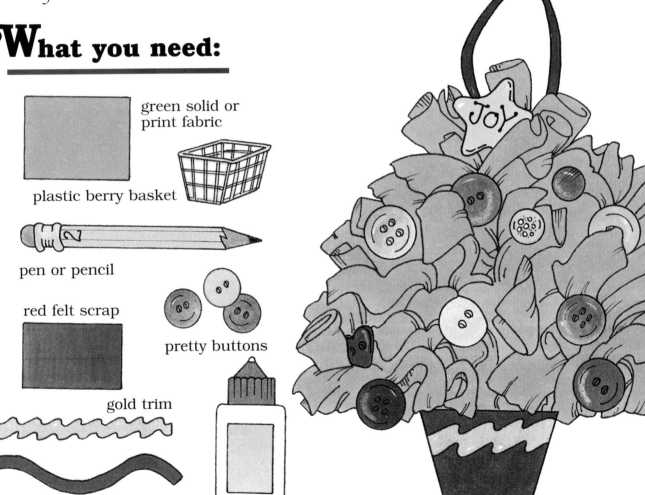

green solid or print fabric

plastic berry basket

pen or pencil

red felt scrap

pretty buttons

gold trim

thin red ribbon

white glue

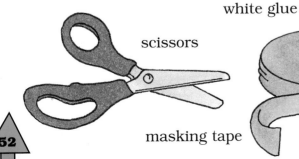
scissors

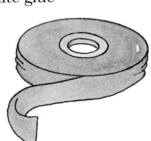
masking tape

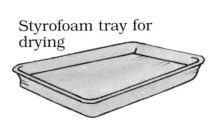
Styrofoam tray for drying

What you do:

1 Cut the edges off the berry basket to about halfway down. Cut a triangle-shaped tree with a trunk out of the bottom of the basket. Keeping the edges on the basket will make it easier to work on and dry the project.

2 Cut about twenty-five 1½-inch (3.8-cm) squares of green fabric. Use a pen or pencil to poke the center of each fabric square through a hole in the triangle tree shape. Fill the entire triangle with fabric—but not the base of the tree. Drizzle glue over the back of the project to secure the fabric and let it dry on the Styrofoam tray.

3 When the glue has dried, trim away the edges of the basket that were left.

4 Cut a front and back base for the tree from the red felt. Put a piece of masking tape on the inside of the front and back pieces, then glue them together over the plastic base of the tree. Glue a strip of gold trim across the front of the base to decorate it.

5 Cut a 4-inch (10-cm) piece of red ribbon. Thread one end through the top of the tree and tie the two ends together to make a hanger for the ornament.

6 Decorate the tree by gluing on lots of colorful buttons. Put a small piece of masking tape on the back of each button to create a better gluing surface.

You might have another idea for how you would like to decorate the tree.

53

Christmas Candy Ball

*Just about anyone would be happy
to receive this yummy gift.*

What you need:

2½-inch (6-cm)
Styrofoam ball

straight pins

bag of twist-wrapped candy

white glue

garland

masking tape

ribbon

scissors

plastic laundry
bottle cap

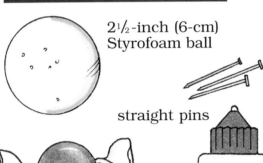

What you do:

1 Turn the cap open-end-up and put masking tape around the open edge to create a better gluing surface. Cover the taped edge with glue. Push the Styrofoam ball into the cap as far as it will go, embedding the glue-covered edge of the cap into the ball.

2 Starting at the bottom of the ball, use a pin to attach the paper at one end of a piece of candy to the ball so that it hangs down over the edge of the lid. Hang candies all the way around the ball, then start a new row above the bottom row. Continue attaching candies until the entire ball is covered.

3 Cut a 2-foot (61-cm) length of garland. Starting at the bottom of the ball, tuck the garland randomly between the candies, going around and around the ball and working toward the top. If you need more garland, just cut another piece. The garland should stay in place between the candies without additional pins, but you can use more pins if you feel they are needed.

4 Tie a ribbon in a bow around the lid just below the candy ball.

5 This can be done with any kind of candy that is wrapped in cellophane that is twisted at both ends.

Yum-yum!

Photo Elf Pin

I'm sure your mom would love it if you made her one of these pins to wear on her coat this Christmas season.

What you need:

old knit glove or mitten in red, white, or green

white glue

wire or pipe cleaner piece

1-inch (2.5-cm)-wide plastic cap

scissors

masking tape

pin backing

cotton ball

trim

jingle bell

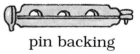

photo with your face about 1 inch (2.5 cm) around

What you do:

1 Glue the cotton ball inside the cap to fill it. Cut the picture of your face from the photo and glue it over the cotton ball.

2 Cut the thumb off the mitten or glove to make the hat. Attach the jingle bell to the tip of the thumb by threading a piece of pipe cleaner or wire through the top of the bell and the knit fabric, then twisting the two ends together. Trim off any extra pipe cleaner or wire from the ends.

3 Roll the cut end of the thumb up to form a brim for the hat. Put glue on the top part of the cap and photo, then slip the hat on over the glued portion.

4 Glue a band of trim around the hat just above the brim.

5 Wrap the back of the pin back with masking tape to create a better gluing surface. Glue the pin back to the back of the cap.

Now your mom can wear her favorite little "elf" right on her coat collar.

Paper Folds Angel

Here is another great project using old catalogs.

What you need:

catalog with about twenty-four pages

gold glitter

poster paint in skin tone of your choice and paintbrush

pipe cleaner

yarn bits for hair

ribbon

2½-inch (6-cm) Styrofoam ball

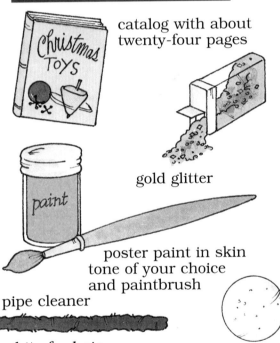

masking tape

hair spray

thumbtacks

aluminum foil

construction paper scrap in matching skin tone

Plus scissors, white glue, and newspaper to work on

What you do:

1 Starting on the first page of the catalog (not the cover), fold the corner of the page down to the center of the catalog so that it forms a triangle. Fold each page of the catalog the exact same way and in the same direction.

2 Paint the Styrofoam ball the skin tone of your choice for the head. Glue yarn bits on the top for hair. Use thumbtacks to make eyes and a mouth for the angel.

3 Push the end of a pipe cleaner into the bottom of the head. Separate the two center pages of the catalog and squeeze glue down the centerfold of the book. Place the pipe cleaner in the glue so that the head rests on the top of the points of the folded pages. Press the two center pages together to hold the head in place.

4 Fold the top of the front and back covers down about 2 inches (5 cm) to form arms for the angel. Cut hands from the construction paper scrap and glue one under the end of each sleeve.

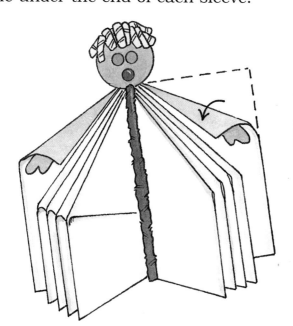

5 Tie a ribbon around the neck of the angel.

6 Tear off a square of aluminum foil. Fold the square in half and cut a wing shape on the fold. Do not cut the fold apart. Open the foil so you have two identical wings. Put a strip of masking tape across the center of the wings to create a better gluing surface. Glue the wings to the back of the angel.

7 Ask a grown-up if you can use some hair spray. If it is all right, spray the sleeves and dress of the angel, then quickly dust with glitter. You can also decorate the angel using glue, but it will not be quite as evenly covered as it is using hair spray.

The size of your angel will depend on the size of the catalog you use.

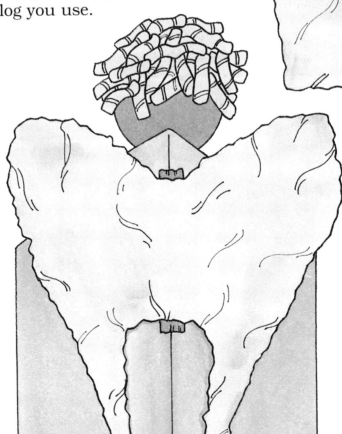

Earring Sweater Guard

You can make this delightful gift quickly and easily.
I bet your grandma would love this one!

What you need:

pretty pair of
old clip-on
earrings

thin trim or ribbon

scissors

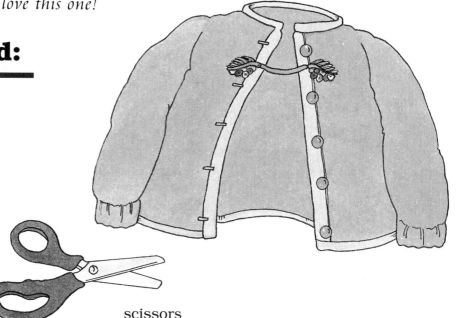

What you do:

1 Cut a 9-inch (23-cm) piece of thin ribbon or trim.

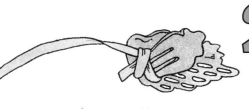

2 Tie one end to the back of each earring. Trim off the extra ribbon or trim on each end.

That is all you do. One earring is clipped to the top front of each side of a cardigan sweater to keep it from slipping off the shoulders. Clip-on earrings can be easily found for very little money at rummage and garage sales.

Bows Christmas Tree

Turn last year's Christmas bows into this year's table decoration.

What you need:

two 4-inch
(10-cm) bows

one 3½
(9-cm)-inch bow

one 3-inch
(8-cm) bow

two 2-inch
(5-cm) bows

white glue

glitter

Styrofoam tray to
work on

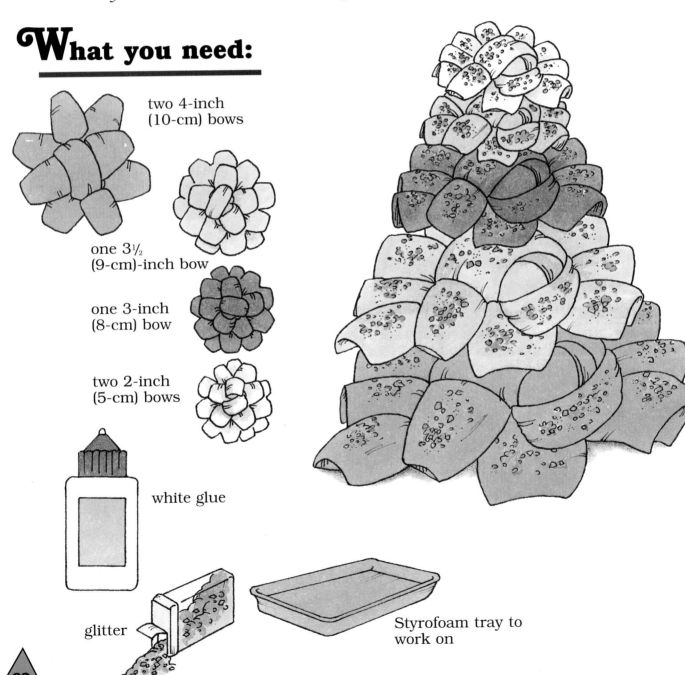

What you do:

1 Stack the bows from largest to smallest to make a tree. Glue the stack of bows together.

2 Cover the edges of the bows with glue and sprinkle with glitter.

This project is so fast and easy you can make a whole forest of trees in no time at all!

About the Author and Artist

Twenty-five years as a teacher and director of nursery school programs has given Kathy Ross extensive experience in guiding young children through crafts projects. Among the more than thirty-five craft books she has written are CRAFTS FOR ALL SEASONS, MAKE YOURSELF A MONSTER, THE BEST BIRTHDAY PARTIES EVER, and CRAFTS FROM YOUR FAVORITE CHILDREN'S SONGS.

Sharon Lane Holm, a resident of Fairfield, Connecticut, won awards for her work in advertising design before shifting her concentration to children's books. Her recent books include SIDEWALK GAMES AROUND THE WORLD, HAPPY BIRTHDAY, EVERYWHERE!, and HAPPY NEW YEAR, EVERYWHERE! all by Arlene Erlbach, and BEAUTIFUL BATS by Linda Glaser.

Together, Kathy Ross and Sharon Lane Holm have also created the popular *Holiday Crafts for Kids* series, *Crafts for Kids Who Are Wild About* series, as well as CHRISTMAS ORNAMENTS KIDS CAN MAKE, CHRISTMAS DECORATIONS KIDS CAN MAKE, and MORE CHRISTMAS ORNAMENTS KIDS CAN MAKE.